Words with
Wrinkled Knees

Also by Barbara Juster Esbensen

Cold Stars and Fireflies: Poems of the Four Seasons

Words with Wrinkled Knees

ANIMAL POEMS

Barbara Juster Esbensen

Pictures by John Stadler

Thomas Y. Crowell

New York

This book
is affectionately dedicated
to my editors,
Barbara Fenton and Kathy Zoehfeld.
They always knew there was
a mysterious "something better"
in hiding.
All they asked of me
was to find it.

B. J. E.

To Aunt Betty and Uncle Lionel

J. S.

Library of Congress Cataloging-in-Publication Data
Esbensen, Barbara Juster.
  Words with wrinkled knees.

  Summary: A collection of poems about words that
express the essence of the animals they identify.
  1. Animals—Juvenile poetry.   2. Children's poetry,
American.   [1. Animals—Poetry.   2. American poetry]
I. Stadler, John, ill.   II. Title.
PS3555.S24W6 1986   811'.54   85-47886
ISBN 0-690-04504-2
ISBN 0-690-04505-0 (lib. bdg.)

Designed by Constance Fogler
1 2 3 4 5 6 7 8 9 10
First Edition

The Animals

ELEPHANT
MOSQUITO
FROG
WHALE
BAT
HIPPOPOTAMUS
SPIDER
LION
SNAKE
GIRAFFE
OWL
KANGAROO
HUMMINGBIRD
PORCUPINE
SEAHORSE
CROW
WOLF
CAMEL
CENTIPEDE
PENGUIN
DINOSAUR

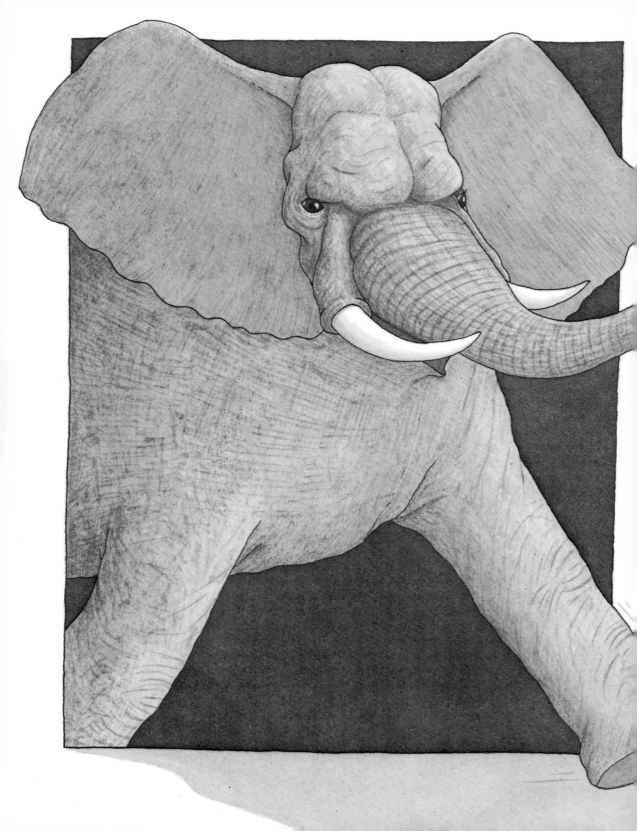

The word is too heavy
to lift   too cumbersome to
lead through a room filled with
relatives or small
glass trinkets

E L E P H A N T

He must have invented it
himself. This is a lumbering
gray word   the ears of it
are huge and flap like loose
wings   a word with
wrinkled knees and toes
like boxing gloves

This word   E L E P H A N T
sways toward us   bulk
and skull-bones filling up
the space   trumpeting
its own wide name
through its nose!

Thin as hairs the letters
whine apart   regroup
M O S Q U I T O   a loose
cloud that swarms
above your head   Your blood
calls   Stilettos at the ready
they zero in for the
kill

Put up screens   close
the windows   Somebody
left the dictionary
open!

1412

MOSQUITO

Touch it with your
pencil
Splat!   The word lands   wet
and squat
upon the page   F R O G

Feed it something light
with wings   Here's one!
Tongue flicks   bright
wing   caught!
Small poem
gone

An evenly balanced
word   W H A L E
it floats
lazily on the page
or dives straight down
to the bottom and beyond
all breath held   held
held   then whoooosh!
The   A   blows its top
into the sun!   W H A L E
serene
sings to us   wet
green sounds from the deepest
part of the alphabet

Every night
a short word
covered with fur   mouth open
flies
out of dark libraries

All day it hangs
upside-down in the card
catalog   under   B

But at sundown   B A T
by the hundreds
leaves the gloomy
pages
of mystery books   crawls
out of damp bindings
and   g l i d e s   into the night air
shaking itself free
of the trailing old words
DRACULA   BLOOD   FANG...

Here is a word
H I P P O P O T A M U S   It sinks
if you look at it   sinks
into mud at the bottom
of warm rivers

At the front end
only the eyes bulge up
The back of this word
drowns in rivertide   Waters curl
around   swirl over
POTAMUS   the part
that looks like a city bus
submerged

This word heaves itself
onto riverbanks   waddles
down the shore   squelches
the mud with its ten-ton
feet   When it yawns
all twelve letters
can fit in   hip
to   hip   to   hip . . .

Her silken name
woven   fine as light
is fastened to the edges
of the page

Where she spins
the word hangs   a letter
at a time   S P I D E R
sticky   anchored against
the wind's breath   waiting

Eight-legged spinner word
swift-running   weaver word
fast-biting   tight-wrapping
get-the-broom-quick   word
S P I D E R !

The name opens wide
as soon as you
speak it   L I
O N   Jaw unhinges
teeth flash white
sharp   against all that
red

From all the best possible
choices   FLEA   TOAD
PEACOCK   he picked this
for himself   L I O N
the only one he could say
while   ROARING!

The word begins to
hiss as soon as the first
letter
goes on   S
s-s-s-s-s-s   forked tongue flickers
Hard eyes stare

Already the rest of the poem
shrinks back from
his narrow speed   The paper
draws in its breath   S N A K E
loops around the pencil
slides
among typewriter keys   slips
like a silk shoelace
away

Quietly nibbling
sneezing now and then
(because of the dust)   this word
munches on the leaves
of books lined up
on the topmost shelves
of high-ceilinged libraries
in the oldest
neighborhoods
in town

G I R A F F E

The whole word has been spray-painted
golden brown through a large
net   The pattern   (light
and shadow filtered through dirty
windows)   protects it
from sharp-eyed
librarians   who think they hear
someone eating paper
high above their heads

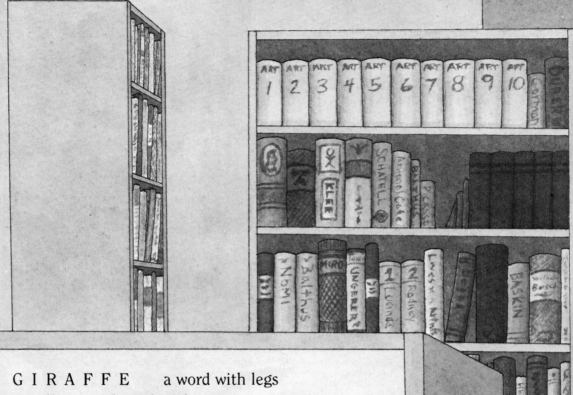

G I R A F F E   a word with legs
so tall   with neck so long
it has never seen
its knees!

A shy word   G I R A F F E   might
take its favorite
food   right from your hand
Offer it a bite of
STEEPLE   TOWER   STRATOSPHERE   and
maybe it will follow you home

If you want to keep   G I R A F F E
in your room
you only need to take
the roof
off the house!

What a moonstruck
word   O W L !
Such round yellow lamps
for eyes   and the hoot
built into the name

Beaked and taloned
it leaves the page
at dusk   When blue light
turns to shadow
and wind moves
the empty paper   this word
O W L
opens soundless wings
s a i l s   o u t
to where the smallest letters
cower in the dark

This big word has
springs
in its tail
and a trampoline
under its feet

K A N G A R O O
comes bounding in
with a bright-eyed
face
in the pocket   two words
for the price of one!

BIG K A N G A R O O   sailing up
little   k a n g a r o o
peering   down
What a ride!   Every slow-motion
jump
washes their ears
with sky!

Glimpse this word   its clockwork
parts   where blossom
intersects with air   A tiny
feathered engine   HUMMINGBIRD
the name and the whirr
are one   Its colors
blur on the page

HUMMINGBIRD   zigzag
stitcher of sky to flower
hemming the edges of gardens
sewing the honey
in

The word comes shambling in
bristling
with a thousand pens
fiercely attached

P O R C U P I N E

Slow-moving   close
to the page   the word
waddles
down the lines

They say   P O R C U P I N E
can shoot his quills   but
he can't   They say
he didn't use a quill
to write this poem
but
he did!

You must read
this word under water
under
wavering nets of cool
light
A vertical word

S
E
A
H
O
R
S
E

with its fragile head   blown
from glass   a curled tail
beneath   The eyes   serious
almost have lashes   blink
No one races here   no crowds cheer

S
E
A
H
O
R
S
E

gentle   upright swims
toward us   We can barely hear
the whinny

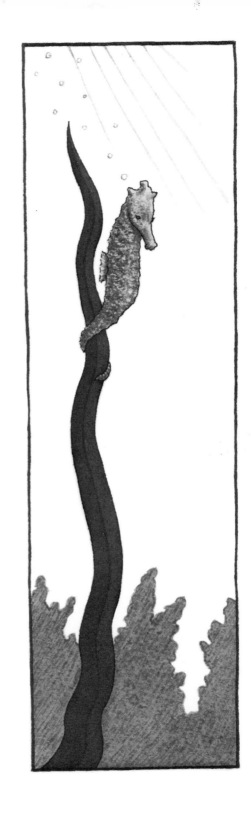

Use your blackest
ink   to print this noisy
word   C R O W

Each letter
flapping and cawing
tumbles out of the sky
crowds down on the page
beak open   neck
s t r e t c h e d

The eyes glitter   If there is
anything worth stealing
in this poem   C R O W
will find it   If
there is anything
dead
in these lines
C R O W
will pick its bones
clean

As soon as you say this word
snow begins to fall

W O L F

A shadow-word   undefined
as fog   it slips behind
sketches of dark pines
and birch trunks
its footprints quick
on the snowy page

W O L F

Whenever you say this word
a little girl fastens her red
cloak   and hurries along
the path

Muzzle turned
to the north wind
W O L F   runs
through the penciled woods
a winter moon
caught in its eyes

Tonk-tank!   Do you hear
bells?   A word
is coming toward us
in long lines   a caravan
of it moving closer
from pages
where heat shimmers
above the dry
paragraphs   and a million
letters are whirled
into shifting dunes

C A M E L

A swaying
spitting
loose-footed word   C A M E L
can go for weeks
never thirsty   plodding
through the deepest   driest
longest books ever written

Chewing on the words
SPRING   WELL   OASIS
C A M E L   stores up
all the water it needs
right between   C A
and   E L   in
M!

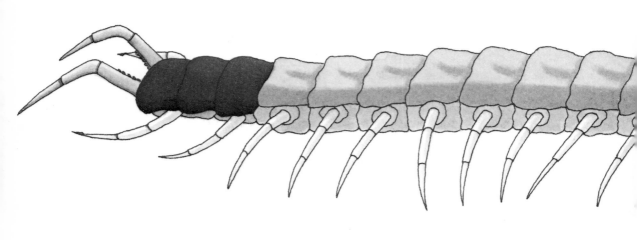

How many legs in the word

C E N T I P E D E ?

One hundred move together
rippling this long word
C E N T I P E D E   from one
page to   the   next
coming dangerously close
to the word
M E !

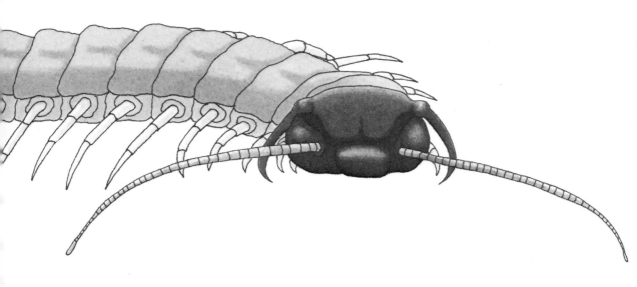

At first
you won't recognize
this word sitting snug
in red underwear
at the bottom of the frozen map

Its feet
in little black slippers
are neatly crossed
Smoke
rises from a pipe   A wrinkled
suit
hangs on a peg   The iron
is heating

P E N G U I N   Best-dressed word
in the world atlas!

Soon it will waddle to work
Look for it
at the Snow Queen Cafe
where the chairs
are carved from blue ice
and snow sifts down
on the band
playing "Jingle Bells"
under a freezing moon

If you beckon it
this word   P E N G U I N
will come skating up
tray held high   skid
to a stop
and bring you a
Snow Queen Special — ANTARCTICA
in a frosted glass!

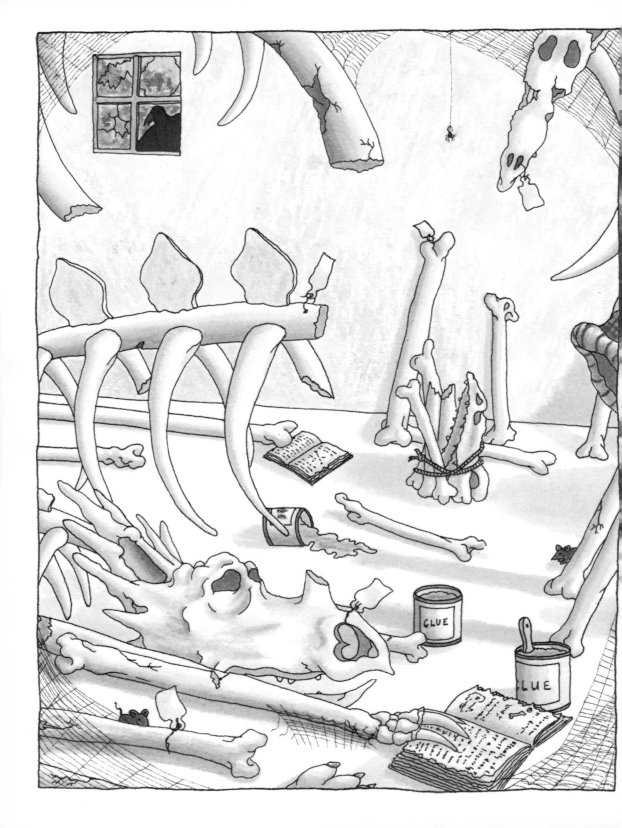

Final edition   In the index
under   D I N O S A U R
we find only
the out-of-print
bones

Once they were
a many-volume set   TRICERATOPS
and   BRONTOSAURUS   lived there
TYRANNOSAURUS REX   roamed
among the footnotes

In a back room
a few large books
remain   spines broken
and faded paper torn
A few legbones lie
scattered among the gluepots
beyond repair

D I N O S A U R   the ancient
lizard word   without
a publisher   copyright
expired